MAKING
THE AMERICAN PROMISE

Historical Geography Workbook
Volume I to 1877

MARK NEWMAN
University of Illinois at Chicago

Bedford Books **M** Boston

PREFACE

Though historians disagree on many things, consensus exists on one important issue: We study and teach change over time and space. Not surprisingly, history has not been immune to the forces of change. The discipline is in the midst of a deep-rooted and substantial reform movement that is well known to history teachers. In teaching, the trend is toward a more student-centered model that uses a variety of interactive methods. The idea is to directly involve students in the learning process and thus enable them to acquire the knowledge, understanding, and skills they need to succeed in college and life.

In recent years, publishers have contributed to history education reform by expanding textbook coverage of different peoples and including special sections that allow more in-depth exploration of relevant topics. They have also surrounded the textbooks with an array of ancillaries that extend learning by helping instructors better engage their students in interactive exercises. Those old, familiar resources, maps, have assumed greater importance because they are such versatile tools. They not only supply a spatial context for content, showing who did what, where and when, but help students develop important skills needed to study history effectively. Also, students like maps.

Mapping The American Promise offers a novel approach to the use of maps in history instruction. The sixty-four workbook exercises explore maps included in the text on three levels: reading the map, connecting the information in the map to content in the chapter, and exploring the map to extend learning. Some activities show students how to manage large amounts of diverse information by having them organize data into tables, charts, timelines, or chronologies. Some place students in historical situations and ask them to make decisions, while others can be used to engender lively discussion in the classroom. An answer key is available so you or the student can check the work.

My hope is that this map workbook will stimulate student interest in history and increase student knowledge and understanding of the historical process by developing skills in reading and note taking, observation and visual analysis, critical thinking and managing information, and writing. To paraphrase the motto of an old television show, American history and maps have many tales to tell, here are sixty-four of the best.

A NOTE TO THE STUDENT

Maps and textbooks. For most of your education, maps and textbooks have been familiar resources. Many of your classrooms were adorned with maps that brightened up the decor and also helped locate the nations and peoples you studied. In virtually every subject, textbooks have been your primary source of information. So a natural connection exists between maps and texts. Maps graphically depict who did what, when, and where, thus supplying the necessary context in which to place the textbook content. In other words, maps help organize information so you can make sense of it. The goals of *Mapping The American Promise* are to build upon this integral relationship and to enable you to use maps with your textbook to enhance your knowledge and understanding of history as well as to stimulate your interest in the subject.

The need to organize and make sense of information is part and parcel of a history education. The goal of studying history is not just to know dates and names—far from it; instead, the idea is to have you study a wide range of facts to analyze their meaning and significance. History strives not just for knowledge, but for understanding. We identify the who, what, how, when, and where of history to figure out the why. History helps explain who we are and how we got here, and offers insight into where we are going.

Maps are important aids in this quest for knowledge and understanding— and have been used in education since antiquity. Inscribed on a clay tablet, the oldest world map is from ancient Babylonia. With other clay tablets that served as the textbooks, the map was used in Babylonian schools to teach children who they were and where they lived in the universe.

Today, maps perform a similar function and much more, because the nature of education has changed. In the past, a major difficulty was a relative lack of readily available information. Today, computers and the Internet, the vast publishing industry, and the media have created a different problem. We are daily bombarded with so much information that it's hard to make sense of everything being thrown at us. Mastering the enormous content of a college history survey class often seems overwhelming. I am sure you recognize that studying history in college requires you to perform at a higher level than in high school in terms of reading, thinking, and writing.

There are two keys to mastering the large amounts of information you encounter in a college history class. One is developing your reading, note-taking, critical thinking, and writing skills so that you select pertinent data, analyze it effectively, and then write your conclusion in a clear, succinct manner. The other is placing the data in a context that facilitates understanding. It is one thing to know about something and another to understand it. History stresses gaining knowledge for understanding.

Maps help you learn history by supplying a visual image that takes in the larger picture of the topic under study. Maps graphically depict a vast amount of diverse information in a variety of ways. By supplying a spatial context to the historical process in a single image, they help you see both the big picture and the important details of various trends and events. But as is true for history generally, you must ask the right questions to open the fruitful dialogue with a map that yields knowledge and understanding.

The sixty-four exercises in *Mapping The American Promise*—two per chapter— directly connect to the content of the text. Generally, they have a three-part format. "Reading the Map" asks you to identify pertinent information on the map. "Connecting to the Chapter" links the map content and context to relevant information in the text chapter. "Exploring the Map" extends the dialogue in numerous and often creative ways, perhaps linking map content to primary sources or the historical question of the chapter, referring to content from past chapters, or challenging you to make decisions about historical events by placing you in the situation depicted on the map.

Other exercises offer different activities related to managing information and developing thinking skills. Constructing a timeline or chronology will help you place historical content in the correct time context. Developing charts and tables teaches you how to organize, categorize, and analyze large amounts of diverse information.

Most journeys require a map to get to the destination. So as you open this workbook and begin your trek through history, use the maps wisely to enjoy your travels and to reach your destination a more intelligent and more competent person than when you began. Good luck!

CONTENTS

ANCIENT AMERICA
BEFORE 1492

Introduction

The theory of plate tectonics holds that the earth's landmasses are continuously moving plates. In addition to causing earthquakes and volcanic eruptions, the movements of these plates have created our continents and our oceans and seas. Map 1.1 depicts a result of this plate movement, called continental drift, that has had enormous consequences for the formation of the earth and human history. See *The American Promise,* page 6.

READING THE MAP

1. Examine Map 1.1 to trace the movement of the earth's landmasses to their location today. Identify the places that were closest together 240 million years ago.

_____

_____

_____

_____

_____

_____

_____

_____

2. Continental drift also created the earth's three oceans. Using the present-day map, identify the continents that determine the boundaries of each ocean.

_____

_____

_____

_____

_____

_____

_____

_____

_____

_____

_____

_____

CONNECTING TO THE CHAPTER

1. According to the chapter, when is it believed that human beings first emerged? Where is it believed they emerged? When did modern humans, *Homo sapiens*, emerge?

   _____

   _____

   _____

   _____

   _____

   _____

   _____

2. Explain how continental drift affected the spread of human beings over the earth.

   _____

   _____

   _____

   _____

   _____

   _____

   _____

   _____

   _____

   _____

   _____

   _____

   _____

   _____

EXPLORING THE MAP

1. What impact do you think continental drift had on the development of people, animals, plants, and disease in the American and Afro-Eurasian landmasses? How might continental drift have affected the eventual meeting of the life forms of these two landmasses after 1492?

   _____

   _____

   _____

   _____

   _____

   _____

   _____

   _____

   _____

   _____

   _____

   _____

   _____

   _____

   _____

   _____

   _____

   _____

   _____

   _____

2. Assuming that the earth's landmasses continue to move, on a separate piece of paper draw a map that shows how the earth might look 240 million years from now.

MAP 1.1
Continental Drift

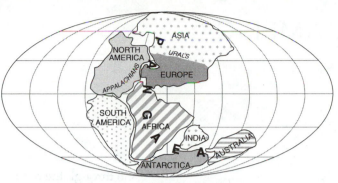

240 million years ago

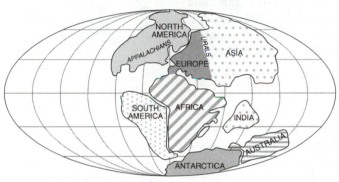

135 million years ago

65 million years ago

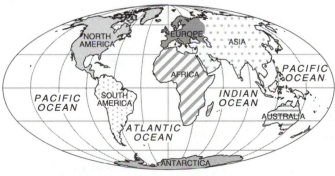

Present-day

ANCIENT AMERICA
BEFORE 1492

Introduction

An estimated 4.5 million peoples, ethnically diverse and speaking more than 200 languages, inhabited North America in approximately 1500. See *The American Promise,* page 26.

READING THE MAP

1. Examine the map and find the area where you live; identify the tribe or tribes that occupied your area in 1500. Now think of any trips you have made in the United States or places you would like to visit. Identify these places on the map and then name the peoples you might have met if these trips had occurred in 1500. On the trips you did take, did you meet any native North Americans?

_____

_____

_____

_____

_____

_____

_____

2. Reflecting the meeting of cultures that occurred in North America, many of our current place-names come from Native Americans.

Go through the map and identify any states and major cities with Native American names.

_____

_____

_____

_____

_____

3. As was true of other peoples throughout the world, some native North Americans occupied the same area for long periods of time, while others migrated to different locations, seeking a better way of life. In looking at the map, you can see that several tribes with the same name appear in different places. Identify these tribes. Is it possible that migration was one cause for this splitting up of larger groups? Do you think these separated groups of the same tribe maintained contact after splitting up?

_____

_____

_____

_____

_____

_____

CONNECTING TO THE CHAPTER

1. One of the best ways to organize the incredibly diverse Native American groups living in North America is by language. Referring to the appropriate pages in the chapter, identify the three major groups living in the Eastern Woodlands regions. On a separate piece of paper, construct a chart that shows the tribes included within each major group mentioned in the chapter, their location, and their primary means of securing food. For example, among the Algonquian, there were the Algonquian–coastal Virginia, who practiced agriculture, hunting, and fishing.

MAP 1.3   Native North Americans about 1500

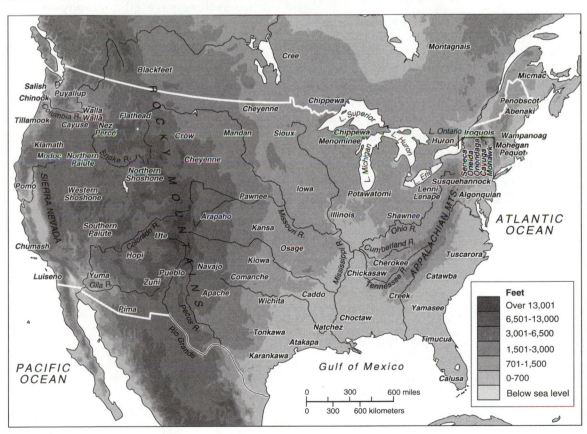

2. The idea of migration was mentioned in question 3 in the previous section. The chapter indicates that in the century or two before 1500, many tribes made new homes in one region in particular. Identify that region, the peoples involved in moving there, and how they made their living. Why do you think they migrated?

_____

_____

_____

_____

3. The chapter suggests that Native Americans employed several means of securing food, including hunting and gathering, fishing, and agriculture. Which groups specialized in agriculture? What crops did they grow? Identify these groups on the map to estimate how widespread agriculture was. Compare and contrast the environments where agriculture was practiced. Which type of temperature—hot or cold—played a more important role in determining whether agriculture occurred or not? Why?

_____

_____

_____

_____

_____

_____

_____

EXPLORING THE MAP

1. An ethnography is a study of a specific ethnic or cultural group that includes information on as many aspects of life and culture as possible, such as language, religion, family structure, inheritance patterns, child-drearing, education, and political, economic, and social systems. Using the map, select a group of people you would like to know more about. Read the brief description of these people or their larger grouping in the chapter and make a list of all the pertinent information. If necessary, refer to the bibliography at the end of the chapter and locate any books on the people. Using the chapter and the selected books, write a two-to-three-page ethnography of these people focusing on their location, the type of community they lived in, gender and other roles for producing food and for determining inheritance, government, and other information.

EUROPEANS AND THE NEW WORLD
1492–1600

Introduction

In the fifteenth century, European mariners, led by the Portuguese, began exploratory voyages that eventually allowed them to master the seas. Their achievements meant that, for the first time ever, people in all parts of the world had access to each other by sea. See *The American Promise*, page 38.

PORTUGUESE EXPLORATION IN PERSPECTIVE

Flowcharts are a good tool to organize a large amount of information and to provide perspective for a topic. Using Map 2.1 and chapter 2, fill out the following chart to place Portuguese exploration in perspective. Then answer the questions following the chart. Use the boldface entries as models.

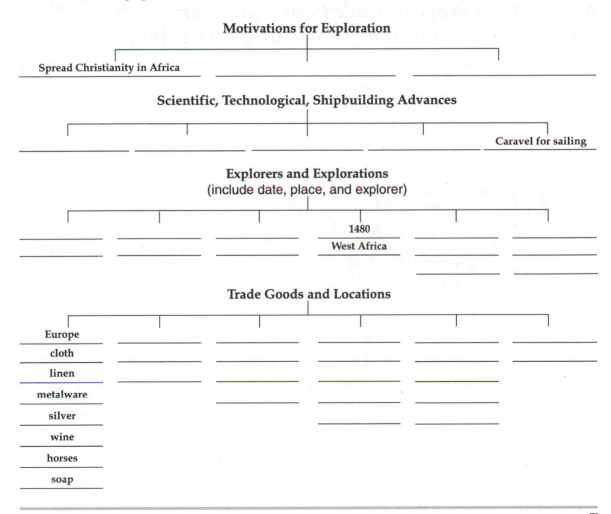

Motivations for Exploration

Spread Christianity in Africa _____ _____

Scientific, Technological, Shipbuilding Advances

_____ _____ _____ _____ Caravel for sailing

Explorers and Explorations
(include date, place, and explorer)

1480
West Africa

Trade Goods and Locations

Europe
cloth
linen
metalware
silver
wine
horses
soap

1. Of the three motivations for exploration, which one do you think was most important, and why?

2. Compare the European, African, and Asian trade goods, and explain who benefited most from the trade opened by the Portuguese.

MAP 2.1 *European Trade Routes and Portuguese Explorations in the Fifteenth Century*

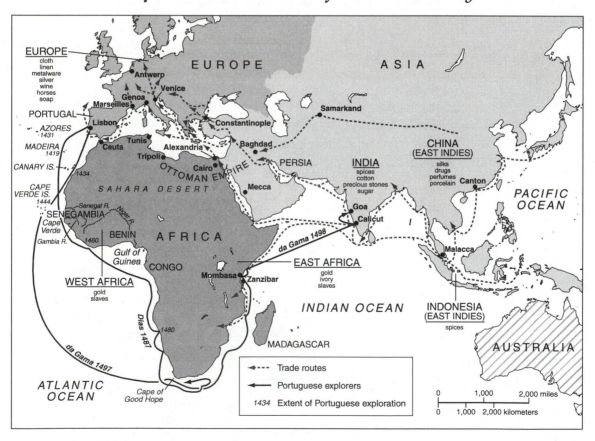

NOTES

EUROPEANS AND THE NEW WORLD
1492–1600

Introduction

The Spanish and, to a lesser extent, the Portuguese were the first Europeans to carve out colonial empires in the Americas. In doing so, they initiated the meeting of Native Americans, Africans, and Europeans in the New World. See *The American Promise*, page 64.

MAPPING TIME

Using chapter 2 and Map 2.3, fill in the following timeline, tracing the course of Spanish colonization from 1492 to 1607. On the left side of the timeline, mark the dates, leaders, and areas explored or states conquered; on the right, mark the dates and names of the cities conquered or founded. Use the boldface entries as models. Then answer the questions on page 12 following the timeline.

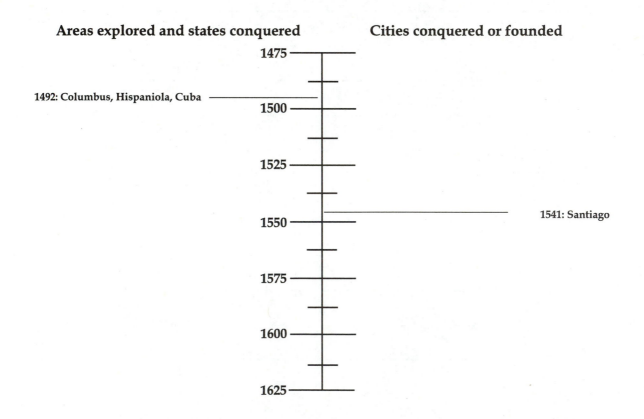

Areas explored and states conquered

Cities conquered or founded

1475

1492: Columbus, Hispaniola, Cuba

1500

1525

1541: Santiago

1550

1575

1600

1625

MAP 2.3 New Spain in the Sixteenth Century

1. Where did Spanish conquest occur first? Where did it spread next?

_____

_____

_____

_____

2. What was the last general area of Spanish colonization?

_____

_____

_____

_____

_____

CONQUEST AND COLONIZATION IN PERSPECTIVE

1. What were the motivations behind the Spanish invasion of the Americas? Which one was most important, and why?

_____

_____

_____

_____

_____

_____

_____

_____

_____

2. Spanish conquest was aided by Native American political conditions in two pivotal areas. What were those areas and political conditions? How did they help Spanish conquest?

_____

_____

_____

_____

_____

_____

_____

_____

_____

3. Using the three motivations for colonization as clues, determine what three functions cities performed in Spanish America.

_____

_____

_____

_____

_____

_____

_____

_____

_____

_____

_____

NOTES

CHAPTER 3

THE SOUTHERN COLONIES IN THE SEVENTEENTH CENTURY
1601–1700

Introduction

One function of maps is to depict geographic conditions. The connection between geography and history was particularly strong in North America in the seventeenth century, when geographic factors played an important role in the meeting of Native Americans, Europeans, and Africans. See *The American Promise*, page 96.

GEOGRAPHY AND MAPS

1. Map 3.1 shows a variety of geographic features. Identify all these features and organize them by land or water. In a case such as "fall line," refer to the chapter for a definition. Here are some other possibly unfamiliar terms:

   * *Piedmont* is an area lying near or at the foot of a mountain range.
   * *Tidewater* is low-lying land typically washed over by flowing tides.

2. Using your answer to question 1, Map 3.1, and chapter 3, answer the following questions.

   a. Examine the map and identify what types of geographic features were favored for English settlement before 1650. Why do you think English settlers chose these sites?

   b. Did any geographic features appear to block English settlement by 1700? If so, what were they and how did they hinder expansion?

MAP 3.1 The Chesapeake Colonies in the Seventeenth Century

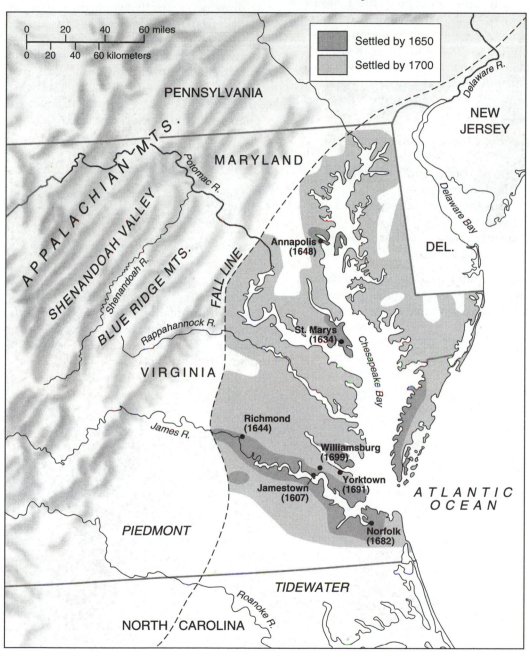

GEOGRAPHY AND SETTLEMENT

1. Prior to the arrival of the English, numerous Algonquian tribes occupied the Chesapeake region. Yet the early English explorers and colonists considered the region an untamed, often savage wilderness. Read the first section of chapter 3 on the Powhatan chiefdom and construct a brief description of these people by including the following information:

   - number of people included in the chiefdom
   - the type of communities they lived in and their locations
   - the means they used to secure food and who performed which tasks
   - any information on other aspects of their lives and culture

Using this description, explain why you do or do not agree with the early English colonists that Virginia was an untamed wilderness.

_____

_____

_____

_____

_____

_____

_____

_____

_____

_____

_____

_____

2. By 1700, English colonization had greatly changed the natural environment of the Chesapeake. Refer to Map 3.1 and chapter 3 to draw two maps that show these changes. In the first map, depict the Chesapeake landscape generally. In the second map, draw a typical tobacco farm and include its specific location in the Chesapeake area. Include a layout of the house, fields, and so on. How did tobacco culture influence the changes on the Chesapeake land?

_____

_____

_____

_____

_____

3. Thinking like a seventeenth-century English settler, decide where to settle in the Chesapeake region. Indicate your location and then on a separate piece of paper explain why you chose it.

Notes

THE SOUTHERN COLONIES IN THE SEVENTEENTH CENTURY

1601–1700

Introduction

The Caribbean was the first American region reached by the Europeans and it remained a major center of activity throughout the colonial era. Developments in the Caribbean often influenced other colonization efforts. For example, plantations based on African slavery originated in the Canary Islands and the Azores of the eastern Atlantic Ocean, but were quickly transplanted to the Caribbean islands. These islands, in turn, became models for slave-based plantation agriculture in the Americas. See *The American Promise*, page 104.

READING THE MAP

1. The Caribbean region was colonized by the Spanish, French, Dutch, and English. Besides Barbados, identify the other English Caribbean islands on the map.

   _____

   _____

   _____

   _____

   _____

   _____

2. Which European country had colonized most of the American continent bordering the Caribbean? Where was the closest mainland English territory?

   _____

   _____

   _____

   _____

3. Place-names often have special significance. For example, because Christopher Columbus mistakenly thought he had reached Asia, the Caribbean region was misnamed the West Indies (as a counterpart to the East Indies—China, and Indonesia). King Charles II of England granted the charter to establish a colony in North America south of the Chesapeake. Looking at the map, identify how the eight men who received the charter thanked the king.

   _____

   _____

   _____

   _____

4. One of the men included in the Carolina charter was a planter from Barbados. How

far was Barbados from the Carolinas? Why do you think Barbadian planter John Colleton sought this charter?

_____

_____

_____

_____

_____

CONNECTING TO THE CHAPTER

Historians have become increasingly aware that regions centered around bodies of water often formed distinctive cultures. Chapter 3 indicates that the society of the Carolina colony was similar to English Caribbean society in many ways.

1. Why was Barbados the jewel of the British West Indies? Why did many English

MAP 3.2 *Carolina and the West Indies in the Seventeenth Century*

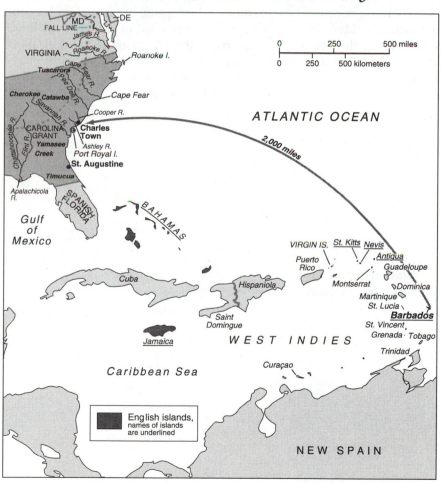

colonists want to leave Barbados in the mid-seventeenth century, and where did they go?

_____

_____

_____

_____

_____

_____

2. In 1700, English officials described Carolina as being in the West Indies, because of its similarities to Barbados. Identify those similarities by describing the economic and social systems of the North American colony and Barbados.

_____

_____

_____

_____

_____

_____

3. What other economic relationships connected Carolina and the English Caribbean islands?

_____

_____

_____

_____

_____

_____

EXPLORING THE MAP

1. One of the more interesting aspects of the founding of Carolina concerned its colonial constitution. One of the colony owners was Anthony Ashley Cooper, Earl of Shaftesbury. Cooper was a friend of philosopher John Locke and hired Locke as his personal secretary. The two men wrote a constitution for Carolina that was never implemented. Locke later had a major impact on American history because ideas he presented in the aftermath of the 1688 Glorious Revolution in England were later used in the American Revolution. Write a two-to-three-page biography of Locke that includes a description of his major ideas and how they were used in the Glorious Revolution and the American Revolution. Try to find a copy of his Carolina constitution and compare his ideas for Carolinian society with his later ideas.

NOTES

THE NORTHERN COLONIES IN THE SEVENTEENTH CENTURY
1601–1700

Introduction

New England was the second region settled by English colonists. The geographic conditions and the Puritan background of the colonists determined how New England developed. See *The American Promise,* page 123.

PLACE-NAMES AND THE MEETING OF CULTURES

The selection of place-names in New England offers much insight into the mentality of the English colonists settling there.

1. From Map 4.1, make a list of the names of the colonies and towns in New England. Referring to chapter 4 and perhaps a map of England in the 1600s, identify at least five names that had European origins and any that came from America. How do the European names and the name of the region show what the English colonists wanted to create in America?

NEW ENGLAND COLONIZATION IN PERSPECTIVE

Referring to Map 4.1 and chapter 4, complete the chart on page 24 to place the colonization of New England in perspective. Use the bold-face entries as a model. Then answer the following questions.

1. What was the primary motivation behind the founding of colonies in New England? How did this motivation affect settlement?

2. Compare the chart on page 24 with the time-line exercise for Map 2.3. How did colonization of New England differ from Spanish colonization in terms of motivation, types of settlements, and types of populations? You may also need to refer to chapters 2 and 4 to answer the question completely.

MAP 4.1 New England Colonies in the Seventeenth Century

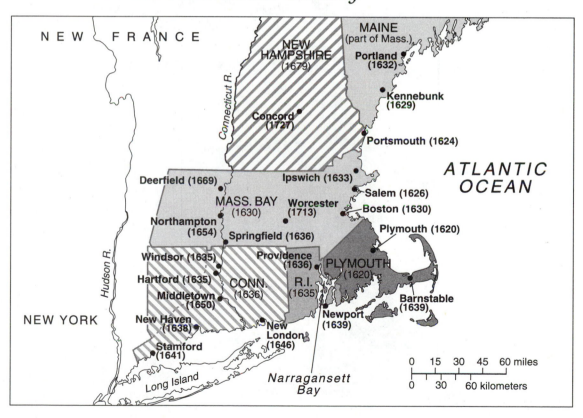

Colony and date of founding	Motivation for founding	Founding of towns in chronological order
Plymouth (1620)	Form separate religious community	Plymouth (1620) Barnstable (1639)

NOTES

THE NORTHERN COLONIES IN THE SEVENTEENTH CENTURY
1601–1700

Introduction

With the founding of Georgia in 1732, the English North American colonies achieved their final form. Ranging along the Atlantic seaboard, the colonies contained more differences than similarities. See *The American Promise,* page 143.

READING THE MAP

1. The colonies were divided into specific regions. Identify these regions and list the colonies by region in chronological order by date of founding.

2. The territorial claims of the colonies generally extended far beyond actual settlement. Which colonies were the most settled and which the least? Was there a connection between extent of settlement and date of founding? If so, what was it?

3. What geographic feature acted as the boundary for colonial territorial claims?

4. What other European nations had territories in North America? Which European nation claimed the most territory? Which European nation had the greatest extent of settlement?

MAP 4.3 American Colonies at the End of the Seventeenth Century

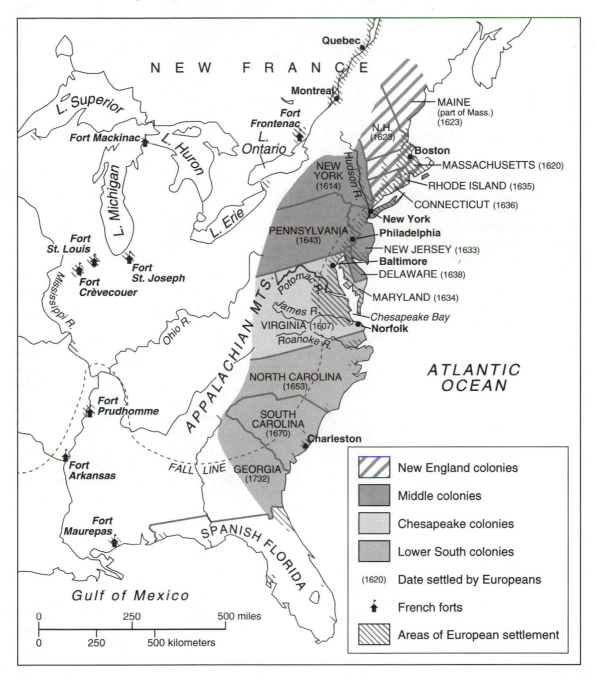

NEW FRANCE

Quebec

Montreal

Fort Frontenac

L. Superior

Fort Mackinac

L. Huron

L. Michigan

L. Ontario

L. Erie

Fort St. Louis

Fort St. Joseph

Fort Crèvecouer

Mississippi R.

Ohio R.

APPALACHIAN MTS.

Potomac R.

James R.

Roanoke R.

MAINE (part of Mass.) (1623)

N.H. (1623)

Boston

MASSACHUSETTS (1620)

RHODE ISLAND (1635)

CONNECTICUT (1636)

NEW YORK (1614)

Hudson R.

New York

PENNSYLVANIA (1643)

Philadelphia

NEW JERSEY (1633)

Baltimore

DELAWARE (1638)

MARYLAND (1634)

Chesapeake Bay

Norfolk

VIRGINIA (1607)

NORTH CAROLINA (1653)

ATLANTIC OCEAN

SOUTH CAROLINA (1670)

Charleston

Fort Prudhomme

Fort Arkansas

FALL LINE

GEORGIA (1732)

Fort Maurepas

SPANISH FLORIDA

Gulf of Mexico

New England colonies	
Middle colonies	
Chesapeake colonies	
Lower South colonies	
(1620)	Date settled by Europeans
	French forts
	Areas of European settlement

0   250   500 miles

0   250   500 kilometers

5. How did the settlement patterns of the French and British differ?

_____

_____

_____

_____

_____

CONNECTING TO THE CHAPTER

1. A variety of factors differentiated the British colonies in North America. Use Map 4.3 and chapters 2 and 3 to construct profiles of the colonial regions indicated on the map. In your profiles, include such characteristics as population (origins, racial composition, class structure), economic system (type of agriculture, trade, other industries, labor system), rural versus urban settlement, type of colonial charter, and type of government. Compare and contrast these profiles to identify similarities and differences.

_____

_____

_____

_____

_____

_____

_____

_____

_____

_____

2. While the map divides the colonies into four regions, can you think of a different organization? On what criteria would it be based? Which colonies would be included in the different categories?

_____

_____

_____

_____

_____

_____

_____

_____

_____

EXPLORING THE MAP

1. One of the most intriguing questions to ask in analyzing a photograph is "What is missing?" Just as the camera lens can capture only part of the entire scene, so maps cannot include everything. Often themes or topics determine the map's features. From your reading and other knowledge, can you tell who is missing from this map? Should they be missing? Explain why you think they should or should not be missing.

_____

_____

_____

_____

_____

NOTES

CHAPTER 5

COLONIAL AMERICA IN THE EIGHTEENTH CENTURY

1701–1760

Introduction

The meeting of peoples in colonial British North America was truly a multicultural affair. The terms *Native American, African,* and *European* identify the origins of the major peoples involved, but these designations do not do justice to the many diverse ethnic and linguistic groups included within these larger headings who interacted in North America. See *The American Promise,* page 156.

READING THE MAP

1. Identify the major ethnic groups identified on Map 5.1. List the thirteen colonies and the ethnic groups living in each colony. What group is missing from the map?

2. In looking at your list and the map, try to identify a pattern of settlement for the various groups. Look for colonies where the map indicates that certain groups outnumbered others or that certain groups seem absent. The map indicates settlement extended from the Atlantic coast to the Appalachian Mountains and beyond. What groups tend to be more numerous in the backcountry areas? Near the coast?

MAP 5.1 Europeans and Africans in the Eighteenth Century

3. Where was African slavery most prevalent?

_____

_____

_____

_____

_____

_____

_____

CONNECTING TO THE CHAPTER

1. The population of the colonies grew dramatically in the eighteenth century. How many people immigrated to the Americas between 1700 and 1776? Break down the percentage of migrants from the ethnic groups indicated on the map to show who came in the greatest numbers. Labor was a major need in the colonies. How was this need met and how did it affect immigration?

_____

_____

_____

_____

_____

_____

_____

_____

2. Migration is often considered to result from two factors. The first factor is conditions present in the original home that are pushing people to leave. The second is con-

ditions present in a new location that pull people there. What "push" factors led people (other than Africans) to migrate to America? What "pulled" people to America?

_____

_____

_____

_____

_____

_____

3. Despite the diversity of peoples and socioeconomic conditions, most English colonists shared three "unifying experiences." What were they?

_____

_____

_____

_____

_____

EXPLORING THE MAP

1. In recent years, historians have discovered much more information about the lives of African slaves. Using chapter 5 and Map 5.1, write a biography of an African slave in the eighteenth century. Begin with the person's birth in Africa and then describe his or her capture, experience on the Middle Passage, sale, and work and personal life as a slave.

Notes

COLONIAL AMERICA IN THE EIGHTEENTH CENTURY
1701–1760

Introduction

By the eighteenth century, a complex system of intercontinental trade had arisen in the Atlantic region. The American colonies were a major center for this trade, both as a source of products and as a market for outside goods. But Atlantic trade clearly defined the types of goods that followed the channels of shipping into and outside the colonies. See *The American Promise,* page 168.

READING THE MAP

1. Identify the major markets for Atlantic trade. Where were they located? What was the significance of the place-names of the African markets?

2. Make a table to chart the flow of goods into and out of England. Trace the stops of the various ships leaving England to identify what goods the English exported where.

Next follow the arrows coming into England and identify the goods imported and where they came from.

3. What were the major ports in the colonies, what colonial regions were they located in, and what goods did they export? What does the export of goods indicate about the types of goods these colonies produced?

CONNECTING TO THE CHAPTER

1. Using Map 5.2, the table you constructed in question 2 in the previous section, and chapter 5, indicate what types of goods were exported from England and what types were imported. Chapter 5 indicates that England's export trade had grown tremendously in the 1700s. How much did export-oriented industries grow in the same period? How did the flow of different types of goods support the growing importance of the export trade?

_____

_____

_____

_____

_____

_____

MAP 5.2   *Atlantic Trade in the Eighteenth Century*

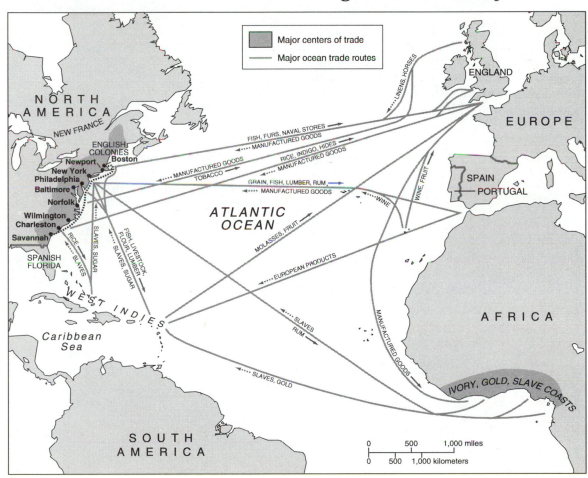

2. According to chapter 5, what were the English colonial trade policies and how did these policies affect the Atlantic trade?

_____

_____

_____

_____

_____

_____

_____

3. From Map 5.2 and chapter 5, what was the Middle Passage? Why did it have this name and who was involved in it? Describe the conditions of the Middle Passage.

_____

_____

_____

_____

_____

_____

_____

EXPLORING THE MAP

1. Following the routes shown on the map, trace one ship's voyage from England and back. Using each continent as a stopping place, identify the geometric shape that the ship's voyage made. What does the shape indicate about the Atlantic trade and what motivated the configuration?

_____

_____

_____

_____

_____

_____

_____

_____

2. Given the character of the Atlantic trade, where would industrialization be likely to arise first—Africa, North America, or England? Why?

_____

_____

_____

_____

NOTES

CHAPTER 6

THE BRITISH EMPIRE AND THE COLONIAL CRISIS
1754–1775

Introduction

By the mid-eighteenth century, European colonization in North America had progressed to the point where the French pushing east and the British moving west were now in physical contact with each other. The meeting of the French and the British created a tense situation that erupted into the French and Indian War. The conflict was appropriately named because it pitted the French and their Algonquian allies against the Anglo-American colonists, the British army, and a much smaller contingent of Native American allies. See *The American Promise*, page 203.

READING THE MAP

1. By 1750, the Spanish, French, and British had established strong claims and permanent settlements in eastern North America. Locate the British territorial claims. In what present-day areas did they exist? In what present-day area were the French claims? In what present-day areas were claims disputed by the French and the British?

_____

_____

_____

_____

_____

_____

2. If the thirteen British colonies are the focus, it appears that the French claims encircled British territory. But if the focus is enlarged to North America, how would you explain the French situation in one sentence?

_____

_____

_____

3. Refer to Map 1.3 on Native North Americans about 1500 and identify the Native American groups in the Appalachian region that were affected by the expansion of the French and British in the eighteenth century. How do you think they felt about the increasing European expansion on the land? What did they do?

_____

_____

_____

_____

_____

_____

MAP 6.1   European Areas of Influence and the French and Indian War, 1754–1763

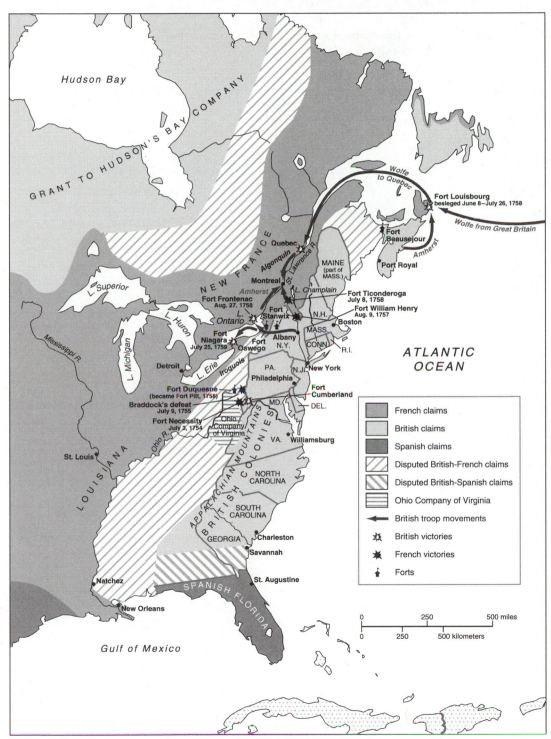

Hudson Bay

GRANT TO HUDSON'S BAY COMPANY

Wolfe to Quebec

Fort Louisbourg
beseleged June 8–July 26, 1758

Wolfe from Great Britain

Amherst

Fort Beausejour

Algonquin

Quebec

MAINE
(part of MASS.)

Port Royal

Amherst

Montreal

L. Champlain

Fort Ticonderoga
July 8, 1758

Fort Frontenac
Aug. 27, 1758

Fort Stanwix

Fort William Henry
Aug. 9, 1757

Boston

L. Superior

L. Ontario

N.H.

Fort Niagara
July 25, 1759

Fort Oswego

Albany
N.Y.

MASS.

CONN

L. Huron

L. Michigan

R.I.

ATLANTIC OCEAN

Detroit

L. Erie

Iroquois

PA.

N.J. **New York**

Mississippi R.

Philadelphia

Fort Duquesne
(became Fort Pitt, 1758)

Fort Cumberland

Braddock's defeat
July 9, 1755

MD.

DEL.

Fort Necessity
July 3, 1754

Ohio Company of Virginia

Ohio R.

VA. **Williamsburg**

St. Louis

L O U I S I A N A

A P P A L A C H I A N   M O U N T A I N S

B R I T I S H   C O L O N I E S

NORTH CAROLINA

SOUTH CAROLINA

GEORGIA

Charleston

Savannah

Natchez

S P A N I S H   F L O R I D A

St. Augustine

New Orleans

Gulf of Mexico

▨	French claims
▨	British claims
▨	Spanish claims
▨	Disputed British-French claims
▨	Disputed British-Spanish claims
▤	Ohio Company of Virginia
←	British troop movements
✹	British victories
✸	French victories
♟	Forts

0		250		500 miles
0	250		500 kilometers	

THE FRENCH AND INDIAN WAR
IN PERSPECTIVE

Using Map 6.1 and chapter 6, construct a chronology of the French and Indian War in the following table. Then use the chronology and chapter 6 to answer the questions following the table.

Date	Battle	Victor

1. Who seemed to be winning the war in the early years? What was the turning point in the war?

2. Why did the British win the French and Indian War?

NOTES

THE BRITISH EMPIRE AND THE COLONIAL CRISIS
1754–1775

Introduction

The French and Indian War was a major turning point in colonial history. The withdrawal of the French from the continent profoundly altered the political and economic balance of power. See *The American Promise*, page 206.

READING THE MAP

1. Identify the European nations claiming land in North America in 1750 and the location of those lands. Who else had a land grant in North America? Do you know what European nation made this grant?

2. By 1763, the European claims had changed drastically. Who were the big winners? Who were the big losers? Which European

nation seemed to have no involvement in the changes?

CONNECTING TO THE CHAPTER

1. While Native American land claims are missing from both maps, their concerns were addressed by the Proclamation Line of 1763. What was the goal of the Proclamation Line of 1763? What geographic feature did it follow? Why did the British issue the proclamation and how did the American colonists respond to it?

MAP 6.2 North America before and after the French and Indian War, 1750–1763

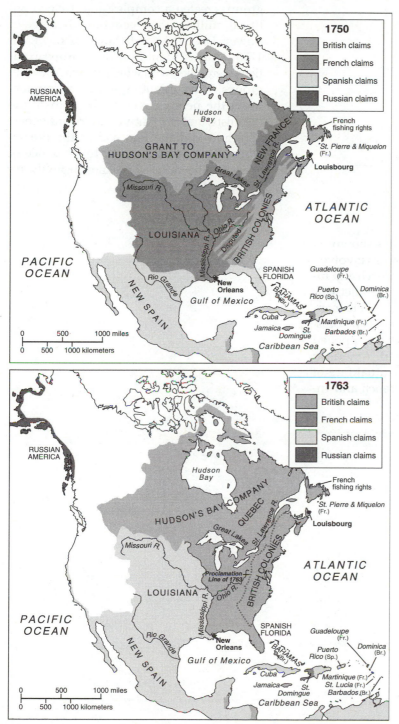

2. Why did Spain get Louisiana from the French?

_____

_____

_____

_____

_____

_____

_____

_____

3. Louisbourg is one of two cities shown on the map. Though Louisbourg was involved in military action during the French and Indian War, its fate in an earlier conflict was equally important. In what previous conflict between England and France had Louisbourg been involved, and what happened after that war that worried American colonists? What was the eventual fate of Louisbourg following the French and Indian War?

_____

_____

_____

_____

_____

_____

_____

_____

_____

_____

_____

EXPLORING THE MAP

1. The links between the competing European nations and the various Native American groups created a complex, intertwined political, military, and economic balance of power. Describe the balance of power in 1750—that is, identify which European nations were allied with which Native American groups. There might be some overlapping. From the perspectives of the British, the colonists, and the Native Americans generally, how did the removal of the French from North America alter this balance of power? Who suffered the most from the removal of the French?

_____

_____

_____

_____

_____

_____

_____

_____

_____

_____

_____

_____

_____

_____

NOTES

CHAPTER 7

THE WAR FOR AMERICA
1775–1783

Introduction

The American Revolution pitted the well-trained, experienced British army against the militia-oriented American forces. Between 1775 and 1778, in a war waged primarily in the North, George Washington created a professional American army and fought the British to a standstill. Battles occurred in several theaters, in the area from Philadelphia to Quebec. See *The American Promise*, page 254.

MAPPING TIME

1. Using the boldface entries as models, complete the following timeline of the major battles between 1775 and 1779. Include the names and dates of the battles. Then answer the questions following the timeline.

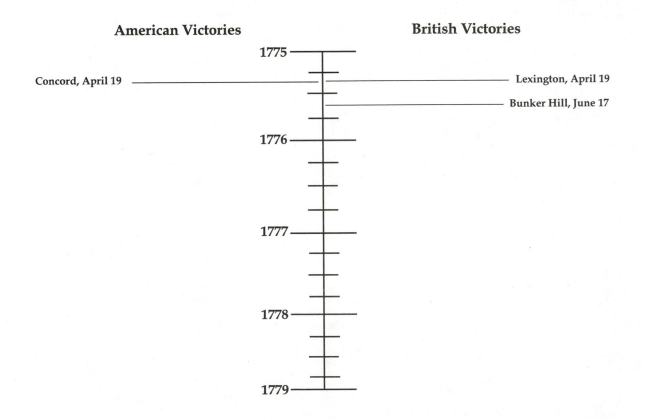

American Victories		British Victories
Concord, April 19	1775	**Lexington, April 19**
		Bunker Hill, June 17
	1776	
	1777	
	1778	
	1779	

MAP 7.1   The War in the North, 1775–1778

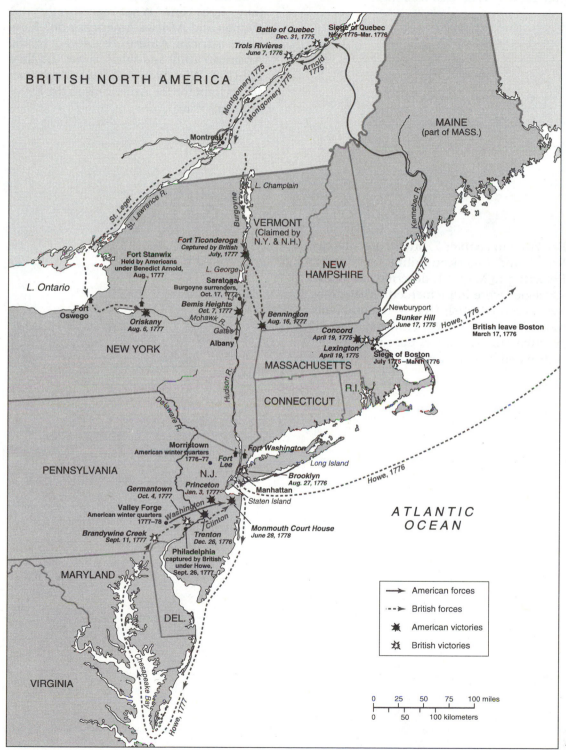

Battle of Quebec
Dec. 31, 1775

Siege of Quebec
Nov. 1775–Mar. 1776

Trois Rivières
June 7, 1776

Arnold 1775

BRITISH NORTH AMERICA

Montgomery 1775

Montgomery 1775

Montreal

St. Leger

St. Lawrence R.

L. Champlain

Burgoyne

MAINE
(part of MASS.)

Kennebec R.

VERMONT
(Claimed by
N.Y. & N.H.)

Fort Ticonderoga
Captured by British
July, 1777

Fort Stanwix
Held by Americans
under Benedict Arnold,
Aug., 1777

L. George

NEW
HAMPSHIRE

Arnold 1775

L. Ontario

Fort
Oswego

Saratoga
Burgoyne surrenders,
Oct. 17, 1777

Bemis Heights
Oct. 7, 1777

Mohawk R.

Oriskany
Aug. 6, 1777

Gates

Bennington
Aug. 16, 1777

Newburyport

Bunker Hill
June 17, 1775

Howe, 1776

British leave Boston
March 17, 1776

NEW YORK

Albany

Concord
April 19, 1775

Lexington
April 19, 1775

MASSACHUSETTS

Siege of Boston
July 1775–March 1776

Hudson R.

R.I.

CONNECTICUT

Delaware R.

Morristown
American winter quarters
1776–77

Fort Washington

Fort
Lee

Long Island

PENNSYLVANIA

N.J.

Brooklyn
Aug. 27, 1776

Manhattan

Howe, 1776

Germantown
Oct. 4, 1777

Princeton
Jan. 3, 1777

Staten Island

ATLANTIC
OCEAN

Valley Forge
American winter quarters
1777–78

Washington

Clinton

Monmouth Court House
June 28, 1778

Brandywine Creek
Sept. 11, 1777

Trenton
Dec. 26, 1776

Philadelphia
captured by British
under Howe,
Sept. 26, 1777

MARYLAND

DEL.

Chesapeake Bay

Howe, 1777

VIRGINIA

→	American forces
⇢	British forces
✶	American victories
✵	British victories

0   25   50   75   100 miles

0   50   100 kilometers

How would you assess the military situation in 1778? Who was winning?

_____

_____

_____

_____

_____

_____

_____

_____

2. Referring to chapter 7, briefly describe the British and American military strategies. Referring to Map 7.1, describe how these strategies were implemented. What problems did the British face? What problems did the Americans face? How did these respective problems affect the success of the British and American military strategies?

_____

_____

_____

_____

_____

_____

_____

_____

_____

_____

_____

_____

3. How did African Americans and women contribute to the war effort? What side did they fight on? What specifically did women and African Americans do? How many African Americans served in the American army and what battles did they fight in? Why would African American slaves fight for the Americans in the Revolutionary War?

_____

_____

_____

_____

_____

_____

_____

_____

_____

_____

_____

_____

_____

_____

_____

_____

_____

_____

_____

NOTES

THE WAR FOR AMERICA
1775–1783

Introduction

The American revolutionaries not only had to fight the British military, but they also faced opposition from Native Americans, African slaves, and colonists loyal to the crown. See *The American Promise*, page 257.

READING THE MAP

1. Identify the areas where support for the Revolution was strong. Where were the loyalist strongholds? What areas were contested?

2. Where were the Native Americans either loyalist or neutral?

3. In examining the respective strength of the rebels and the loyalists, can you determine who seemed to have the upper hand? If the Native Americans are included, how does the balance of power change?

Connecting to the Chapter

1. According to chapter 7, who was likely to be a loyalist, and why?

MAP 7.2   *Loyalist Strength and Rebel Support*

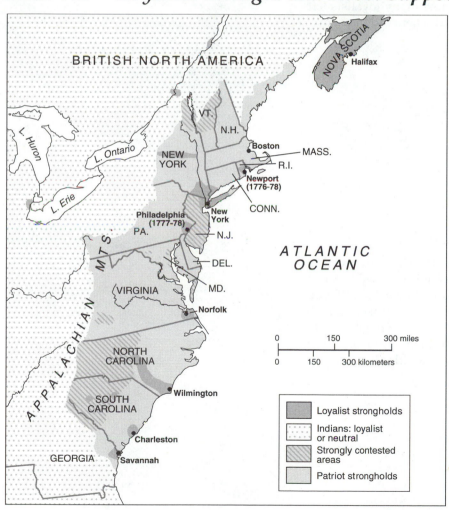

BRITISH NORTH AMERICA

NOVA SCOTIA
Halifax

L. Huron

L. Ontario

L. Erie

VT.

N.H.

NEW YORK

Boston

MASS.

R.I.

Newport (1776-78)

CONN.

Philadelphia (1777-78)

New York

PA.

N.J.

DEL.

MD.

APPALACHIAN MTS.

VIRGINIA

Norfolk

ATLANTIC OCEAN

0   150   300 miles
0   150   300 kilometers

NORTH CAROLINA

Wilmington

SOUTH CAROLINA

Charleston

GEORGIA   Savannah

Loyalist strongholds

Indians: loyalist or neutral

Strongly contested areas

Patriot strongholds

2. How were loyalists treated by the patriots?

_____

_____

_____

_____

_____

3. Loyalists had two choices: stay in the colonies or leave. How many loyalists left the United States and where did they go?

_____

_____

_____

_____

_____

EXPLORING THE MAP

1. Native Americans also were involved in the Revolutionary War. Why would Native Americans side with the British? If you were a British military leader meeting with Native Americans, what arguments would you use to convince them that support of the Revolution was a bad idea?

_____

_____

_____

_____

_____

2. African slaves were also a potent force in the Revolution. How did the revolutionary rhetoric on equality affect the slaves? Most slaves lived in the South. From the map, determine whether their masters were likely to be patriots or loyalists. If you were a loyalist, what argument would you use to convince a slave to remain loyal to the crown? If you were a patriot slaveholder, how would you justify slavery to your slaves? How does your answer to these questions indicate who the Revolution was being fought for?

_____

_____

_____

_____

_____

_____

_____

_____

_____

_____

_____

_____

_____

_____

NOTES

CHAPTER 8

BUILDING A REPUBLIC
1775–1789

Introduction

The creation of the United States and the peace treaty ending the War for Independence raised the issue of the future of western lands, a question that was not finally answered until after the Civil War. At the birth of the nation, however, the issue centered on resolving conflicting land claims among states and between the states and the federal government. See *The American Promise*, page 281.

READING THE MAP

1. The map depicts the confusing situation that existed regarding the states' claims to western lands, but not all states had claims. Which states did not claim western territory? Which states had the largest claims?

_____

_____

_____

_____

_____

_____

_____

_____

2. Which states claimed the same territory, and where was that territory located? What disputed territory became the fourteenth state?

_____

_____

_____

_____

_____

_____

3. Virginia was the first state to cede its western land claims. It relinquished most of its holdings in 1781, but conflicts over private holdings delayed transfer to the national government until 1784. When and in what order did the other states relinquish their claims?

_____

_____

_____

_____

_____

_____

_____

MAP 8.1   Cession of Western Lands, 1782–1802

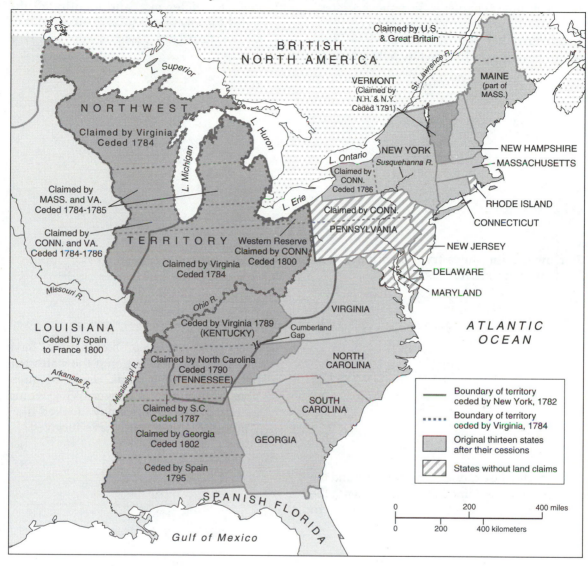

CONNECTING TO THE CHAPTER

1. According to chapter 8, the issue of western lands arose even before independence. When and in what context did the issue first arise? How was this first dispute resolved?

2. How did the states try to legitimize their claims to western lands?

3. How did the experience of the 1760s and the institution of democratic rule influence the decision of Virginia to give up its western lands?

EXPLORING THE MAP

1. Refer to a later map and identify all the states that were eventually carved out of the western land cessions between 1782 and 1802.

2. Speculate on what problems might have arisen for the new nation if the states had not given up their lands. Use these questions to frame your answer: What would eastern North America have looked like? Would the United States have survived?

NOTES

BUILDING A REPUBLIC
1775–1789

Introduction

While the Constitution has proven its utility and durability for more than two hundred years, in 1789, when its ratification was being debated, passage was very much in doubt. See *The American Promise*, page 306.

READING THE MAP

1. Map 8.3 shows that within most states, opinion was divided on the Constitution. Identify the states where there seemed to be a consensus either for or against passage. From the map, would you suggest that more Americans were for or against passage, or was opinion about evenly divided?

_____

_____

_____

_____

_____

_____

_____

_____

2. List the states in order of their passage of the Constitution. Was there any connection between support or opposition shown on the map and the timing of ratification?

_____

_____

_____

_____

_____

_____

_____

_____

3. For passage, nine states had to ratify the Constitution. Examine the chronology of passage. Of those states approving the Constitution after the first nine, which were the most important, and why?

_____

_____

_____

CONNECTING TO THE CHAPTER

Map 8.3 shows the spatial dimension of support and opposition for the Constitution. It also provides some ideas on why opinion in certain states was for or against passage.

1. Using the map and chapter 8, determine where opposition to the Constitution was generally located. What types of people tended to oppose the Constitution? What factors generally motivated opposition?

MAP 8.3 Ratification of the Constitution, 1788–1790

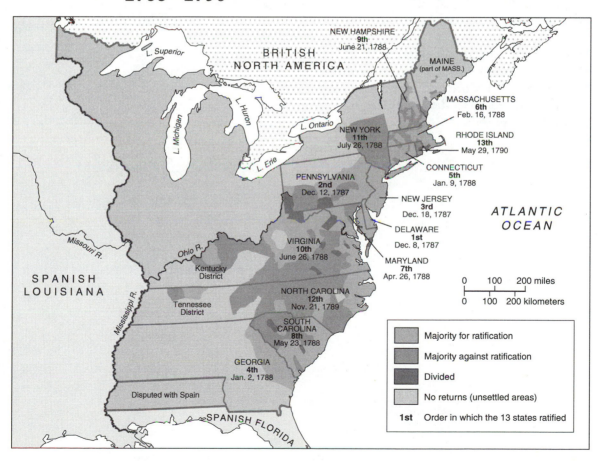

2. Where did those supporting the Constitution generally live? Who generally favored the Constitution? What factors motivated support?

_____

_____

_____

_____

_____

_____

_____

_____

3. Residents of certain states had specific reasons for supporting the Constitution. Why did Delaware and New Jersey support passage? Why did Georgians support the Constitution?

_____

_____

_____

_____

_____

_____

_____

_____

_____

_____

_____

_____

_____

EXPLORING THE MAP

1. The press played a pivotal role in the passage of the Constitution. According to chapter 8, where did the press play the largest role? Why was the press so important in that state? In using the press, the pro-Constitution camp produced seminal work on democratic political philosophy. What was that work and who wrote it? What argument did one of the authors use to counter Antifederalist claims that democratic government was possible only in a small, homogeneous area?

_____

_____

_____

_____

_____

_____

_____

_____

_____

_____

_____

_____

_____

_____

_____

_____

NOTES

CHAPTER 9

THE NEW NATION TAKES FORM
1789–1800

Introduction

In an age when we can cross an entire continent in a few hours by plane or a few days by car, it is difficult to imagine how arduous and time-consuming travel was two hundred years ago. In 1800, a day's travel was measured not in thousands or hundreds, but in tens of miles. See *The American Promise*, page 322.

READING THE MAP

1. Calculate the time it would take to go from New York City to the Mississippi River in 1800 (which, in essence, was how long it took to cross the United States).

2. To gain a sense of a time frame for travel between cities in 1800, plot out a cross-country trip from New York City to New Orleans and back. Travel from New York down the east coast to Charleston and then go west and south to New Orleans. On the return trip, stop in Pittsburgh before coming back to New York City. Estimate the time of each leg of the trip (between cities) and the travel time needed for the entire journey.

CONNECTING TO THE CHAPTER

1. The travel times in 1800 represented a major advance over those in 1790. According to chapter 9, what happened during the 1790s that helped improve travel conditions and speed travel time? When and where did these developments take place? Using a current map as reference, mark the locations and dates of the developments on the map. Who paid for these developments? What other related transportation development occurred in the 1790s?

2. What stimulated the building of roads in the 1790s?

_____

_____

_____

_____

_____

3. How did the absence of roads affect the way western farmers transported their produce to market?

_____

_____

_____

_____

MAP 9.1　Travel Times from New York City in 1800

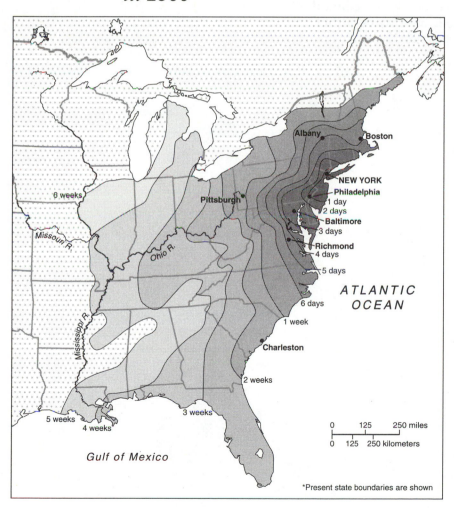

*Present state boundaries are shown

4. What retarded transportation development in the South?

_____

_____

_____

_____

EXPLORING THE MAP

1. Road building acted as a catalyst for development in the United States. How did road building affect the economic and political development of the United States, including settlement and statehood?

_____

_____

_____

_____

_____

_____

_____

_____

_____

_____

_____

_____

_____

_____

_____

_____

2. Who was not pleased with the flurry of road building? Why?

_____

_____

_____

_____

_____

_____

_____

_____

_____

_____

_____

_____

_____

_____

_____

_____

_____

_____

_____

_____

NOTES

THE NEW NATION TAKES FORM
1789–1800

Introduction

Two of the greatest issues confronting the newly reconstituted United States were relations with Native Americans and land expansion. These issues were closely linked and revolved around the question of land ownership—with violence always looming. See *The American Promise,* page 333.

READING THE MAP

1. For the most part, the issues of expansion and Native American land cession initially focused on the area west of the Appalachians in modern-day Ohio. Though the mountain range is not designated on the map, its importance is evident in the tint showing cession from 1750 to 1783. Locate the Appalachians. What line of 1763 ran along the mountains? What was that line's purpose? Looking at the map, determine how well that purpose was met.

2. Map 9.2 shows both the entire territory of the United States and the extent of Native American land cessions. Of the entire area of the United States, estimate how much land had not been given up by Native Americans. Of the area west of the thirteen original states, estimate how much area remained in Native American hands.

3. In what areas or states had land cession occurred between 1750 and 1783? Where did cessions occur between 1784 and 1810?

The issue of land ownership in the early years was a confusing mess and led to a war in the Ohio Territory in the 1790s. The following questions explore the problems of landownership and the course of the war.

MAP 9.2 Western Expansion and Indian Land Cessions to 1810

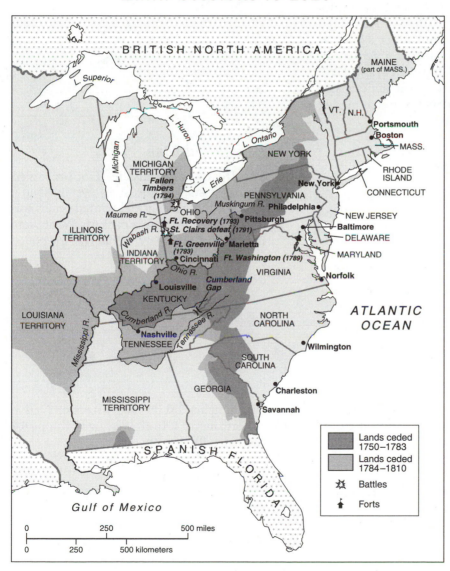

1. Two factors created confusion over landownership. The first was the arrogance of the Europeans, who assumed that Native Americans did not really own the land and that the European nations could thus claim vast expanses of territory. The second cause was conflicting British policies and actions. According to chapter 9, how much territory was involved in this dispute between the United States and various Native American groups? What guarantee had the British given to Native Americans living north of the Ohio River as late as 1768? What had the British given to the United States in the Treaty of Paris in 1783? After the 1783 treaty, what actions had British fort commanders taken that made a volatile situation worse?

_____

_____

_____

_____

_____

_____

_____

_____

_____

2. How much did the population of the United States grow between 1750 and 1790? How did this growth affect the need for western settlement?

_____

_____

_____

_____

3. Profile the two major battles fought in the Ohio Territory in the 1790s. Include as many of the following details as possible: the date and place, American leaders and troop strength, Native American leaders and groups involved, the outcome, and casualties.

_____

_____

_____

_____

_____

_____

_____

EXPLORING THE MAP

1. The Treaty of Greenville (1795) resolved the land issue in Ohio. It also established a policy initiative that the United States followed for more than a century. What were the terms of the treaty? What was the policy initiative?

_____

_____

_____

_____

2. What impact did the treaty have on Native Americans in Ohio? Why was the peace more deadly than the war?

_____

_____

_____

_____

NOTES

CHAPTER 10

REPUBLICAN ASCENDANCY
1800–1824

Introduction

In one fell swoop and $15 million, the Louisiana Purchase doubled the territory of the United States and removed a potentially dangerous enemy from the nation's borders. But President Thomas Jefferson had committed a cardinal sin in buying this property: He purchased it sight unseen. For a number of reasons, including mapping the new lands, Jefferson commissioned several expeditions to explore the Louisiana Purchase. The first and most famous was Meriwether Lewis and William Clark's arduous trip from St. Louis, Missouri, to the mouth of the Columbia River in Oregon Country and back. See *The American Promise*, page 354.

READING THE MAP

1. The territory included in the Louisiana Purchase had specific east–west boundaries determined by prominent geographic features. What were they? The Purchase also created new north–south boundaries that seemed less defined. These north–south boundaries bordered the territories of what European powers?

2. What territory outside the Purchase was claimed by the United States, Great Britain, and Spain?

3. Waterways played an important part in the Lewis and Clark expedition. What waterways were most important, and what role did they play?

4. A continental divide is an imaginary line at the crest of a mountain range that separates rivers flowing to either side of a continent; rivers on one side flow in the opposite direction of rivers on the other side. Though not named on the map, where do you think the continental divide for North America is located? Which way does the Missouri River flow? Which way does the Columbia River flow? How did the river flows affect the Lewis and Clark expedition?

(Question 4 continues) _____

_____

_____

_____

_____

_____

_____

_____

CONNECTING TO THE CHAPTER

1. Though their names are well known, the identities of Lewis and Clark are not. Who were they and how and why were they chosen to lead the expedition? How did Jefferson prepare Lewis for the expedition?

_____

_____

_____

_____

MAP 10.2 *Lewis and Clark and the Louisiana Purchase*

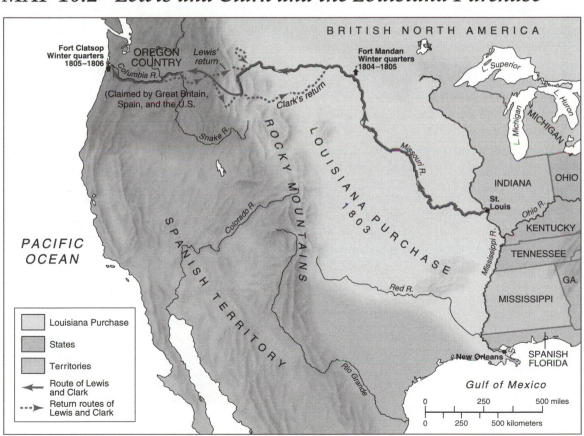

(Question 1 continues) _____

_____

_____

_____

_____

_____

2. What qualifications did Lewis and Clark want for the other members of the expedition? Describe the final crew they assembled.

_____

_____

_____

_____

_____

_____

_____

_____

_____

3. What were the three major reasons for undertaking the expedition?

_____

_____

_____

_____

_____

_____

_____

EXPLORING THE MAP

1. Thomas Jefferson had a well-defined view of the role of government. What was that view, and was his purchase of 828,000 square miles without congressional approval compatible with it? Why did Jefferson make the purchase?

_____

_____

_____

_____

_____

_____

_____

_____

_____

_____

_____

2. After Lewis and Clark, who were the most important members of the crew? Why were they so important? Without the help of Native American groups, what was the likelihood of Lewis and Clark's succeeding?

_____

_____

_____

_____

_____

_____

_____

REPUBLICAN ASCENDANCY
1800–1824

Introduction

Slavery was a recurring issue in early U.S. history, providing flash points for potential conflict and, until the 1850s, opportunities for compromise. Regarding U.S. expansion, the Missouri Compromise established a policy on admission of states that lasted more than three decades. See *The American Promise*, page 373.

READING THE MAP

1. Representation in Congress and political power were pivots on which the political debate over slave versus free states and territories revolved. According to Map 10.4, prior to the Missouri Compromise how many free and how many slave states were there? What did the admission of Missouri as a slave state threaten to do?

2. Does the map show a consistent line dividing the slave and free states? If it does, describe where it is and where it runs. Where was Missouri located in terms of this line?

3. How was slave–free balance achieved?

CONNECTING TO THE CHAPTER

1. Who precipitated the crisis over Missouri? What did he propose, and where did the idea come from?

2. What was the Missouri Compromise, and who proposed it?

3. Looking at Map 10.4, explain who benefited most from the compromise, and why.
Why did the side not benefiting as much
agree to the compromise?

_____

_____

_____

_____

_____

EXPLORING THE MAP

1. If you were a southern slaveholding planter,
where would you favor U.S. expansion,
and why? What does your answer imply
for the future of the United States?

_____

_____

_____

_____

_____

MAP 10.4   *The Missouri Compromise, 1820*

Notes

CHAPTER 11

ANDREW JACKSON'S AMERICA
1815–1840

Introduction

Movement of people, animals, and goods has been a major theme of American history. A corollary theme has been the development of the means of transportation to facilitate this movement. See *The American Promise,* page 387.

READING THE MAP

1. According to Map 11.1, what types of transportation facilities predominated up to 1840?

2. The first road to cross the country was the Post Road, built before 1790. Two other major interstate roads were the National Road and the Great Valley Road. Locate all three roads on the map and identify their endpoints. What was a major difference between the Post Road and the other two? What does this difference indicate about U.S. development?

3. Where were all the major canals located?

CONNECTING TO THE CHAPTER

1. According to chapter 11, who financed most of the transportation improvements? How did states aid these improvements? How did the Supreme Court alter state practices?

MAP 11.1 Routes of Transportation in 1840

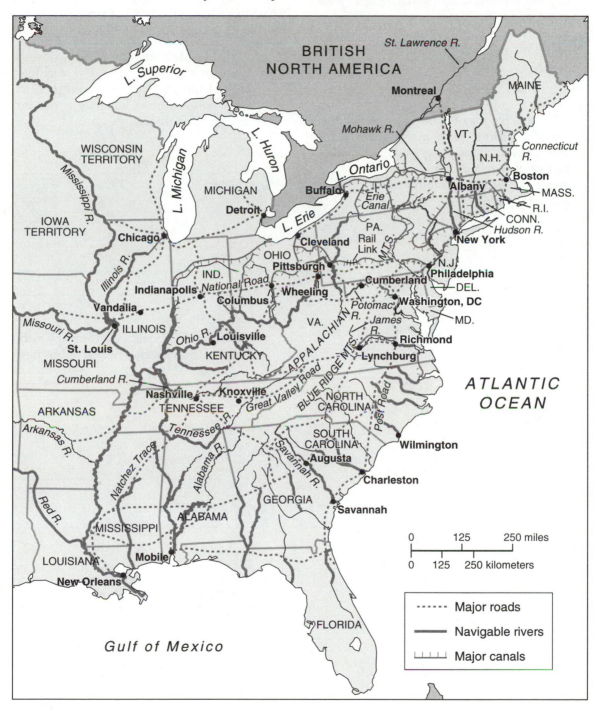

2. What was the major technological advance in water transportation? What dangers were associated with this advance?

_____

_____

_____

3. What was the major canal constructed during this period? How many years did it take to build, how long was it, and what bodies of water did it connect? How did this canal affect economic development and migration?

_____

_____

_____

_____

_____

_____

_____

_____

_____

_____

_____

4. What were the benefits of improved transportation?

_____

_____

_____

_____

_____

EXPLORING THE MAP

1. Write a press release dated 1827 seeking investment for either of the following.

   a. A real estate company seeking investment in a new city on Lake Michigan called Chicago. Explain in your press release how the Erie Canal has made land in Chicago valuable.

   _____

   _____

   _____

   _____

   _____

   _____

   _____

   b. A New York City shipping company extolling how the canal has helped its business.

   _____

   _____

   _____

   _____

   _____

   _____

2. What impact do you think transportation improvements had on Native Americans living east of the Mississippi River?

   _____

   _____

   _____

NOTES

ANDREW JACKSON'S AMERICA
1815–1840

Introduction

The question of where Native Americans fit in U.S. society has vexed government officials, the public, and Native Americans since the founding of the nation. In the 1830s, President Andrew Jackson initiated a new policy of forced removal that led to the relocation of several Native American groups west of the Mississippi River, with tragic consequences for most. See *The American Promise*, page 416.

READING THE MAP

1. Complete the following chart with details about the Native Americans involved in the Indian removal. Use the boldface entries as models.

2. Where were most of the removed Native Americans originally located? What other minority group was affected by the Indian removal?

   _____

   _____

   _____

   _____

3. Through what states did the Trail of Tears go?

   _____

   _____

   _____

Native American Group	Original Home	Date of Cession	New Home
Seminole	**Florida**	**1832**	**Oklahoma**

CONNECTING TO THE CHAPTER

1. Before Andrew Jackson became president, the United States had a rather disjointed Native American policy. How did the federal government view Native Americans and what policy initiatives were undertaken by the government and private groups?

MAP 11.3   *Indian Removal and the Trail of Tears, 1830s*

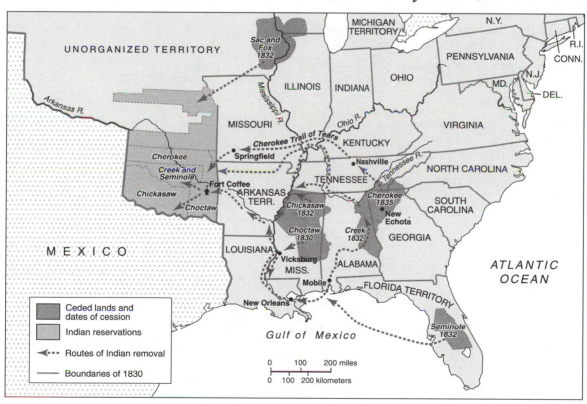

2. How did Andrew Jackson change the government's Native American policies?

_____

_____

_____

_____

_____

_____

_____

_____

_____

_____

EXPLORING THE MAP

The Trail of Tears is one of the most famous and tragic episodes in U.S. history.

1. Write a newspaper article chronicling the experiences of the Cherokee on the Trail of Tears.

_____

_____

_____

_____

_____

_____

_____

_____

_____

2. Was the Cherokee removal legal? Was it moral? Write a newspaper editorial that defends or attacks the removal on legal and moral grounds.

_____

_____

_____

_____

_____

_____

_____

_____

_____

_____

_____

_____

_____

_____

_____

_____

_____

_____

_____

NOTES

CHAPTER 12

THE SLAVE SOUTH
1820–1860

Introduction

In the period before 1860, slavery and cotton defined the South and profoundly influenced the development of the United States. Slavery aroused continuous political and social controversy and debate, while cotton was a bulwark of the economy. See *The American Promise,* page 431.

READING THE MAP

1. Identify the areas with the largest concentration of slaves in 1820 and 1860. Where was slavery most prevalent in 1820? In 1860? Was there any place where slavery declined?

2. Where was cotton production centered in 1820? In 1860?

3. Looking at the map, determine whether the spread of cotton and slavery were related. Was the growth of slavery exclusively tied to the spread of cotton? Why or why not?

CONNECTING TO THE CHAPTER

1. What environmental factors facilitated the spread of cotton?

MAP 12.1 Cotton Kingdom, Slave Empire: 1820 and 1860

Slave population, 1820

Slave population, 1860

Cotton production, 1820

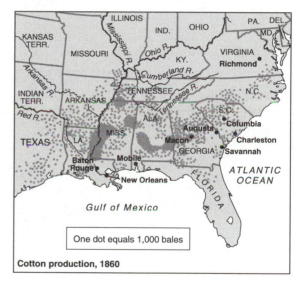

Cotton production, 1860

2. How much cotton was grown on slave plantations by 1860? How much of the world's cotton was produced in the South in 1860? How much of U.S. sales abroad came from cotton by 1840?

_____

_____

_____

_____

3. How much did the slave population grow between 1790 and 1860? What was responsible for that growth, and why?

_____

_____

_____

_____

4. While most slaves worked in agriculture, many did not. How else were slaves employed in cities and in the countryside?

_____

_____

_____

_____

_____

_____

_____

_____

_____

_____

_____

EXPLORING THE MAP

1. Write a journal entry from the perspective of a slave that describes one day in his or her life, either on a plantation or in a city.

_____

_____

_____

_____

_____

2. In most areas of agriculture before 1860, technological invention had provided machines to help in cultivation and harvest. This was not true in cotton production. How do you think plantation owners felt about such inventions? Would planters support experiments in the mechanization of cotton culture? Why, or why not?

_____

_____

_____

_____

_____

_____

_____

_____

_____

_____

THE SLAVE SOUTH
1820–1860

Introduction

The South's economy revolved around agriculture, with certain crops dominating cultivation in various places. See *The American Promise*, page 438.

PUTTING THE SOUTHERN AGRICULTURAL ECONOMY IN PERSPECTIVE

Complete the following chart to profile southern agriculture. Use the boldface entries as models. Then answer the questions following the chart.

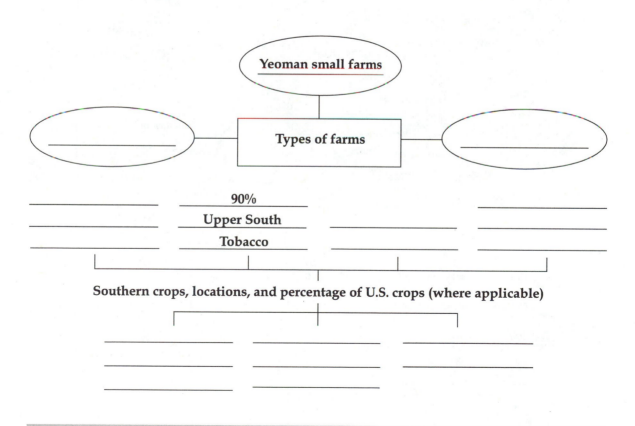

1. What role did the South play in the U.S. economy?

_____

_____

_____

_____

_____

2. Using the chart on page 87 as a model, construct another chart on a separate piece of paper showing the impact that the South's stress on staple crops had on its economic, political, and social development.

MAP 12.2 *The Agricultural Economy of the South, 1860*

NOTES

CHAPTER 13

ABRAHAM LINCOLN'S AMERICA
1800–1860

Introduction

While the United States fought many wars against Native Americans in the drive to expand the nation across the continent, the only major conflict with another colonial or ex-colonial nation was with Mexico between 1846 and 1848. Not surprisingly, the expansionist policy of U.S. President James K. Polk was a major cause of the Mexican War. See *The American Promise*, page 510.

READING THE MAP

1. The Mexican War took place in two general theaters. Where were they? What does the fighting in the Southwest indicate about U.S. war aims?

_____

_____

_____

_____

_____

_____

_____

2. The United States used a multipronged attack strategy to defeat Mexico. Give the leaders' names and describe the move-

ments of the various forces that participated in the main part of the conflict, between the Rio Grande and Mexico City.

_____

_____

_____

_____

_____

_____

_____

3. Excluding Texas, estimate the percentage of territory Mexico lost as a result of the war with the United States.

_____

_____

CONNECTING TO THE CHAPTER

1. The causes of the Mexican War related directly to U.S. expansionist activities. What were these activities?

_____

_____

_____

2. The Mexican War divided the United States along political and sectional lines.

Who was likely to support the war, and why? Who was likely to oppose it, and why?

_____

_____

_____

_____

_____

3. What were the terms of the Treaty of Guadalupe Hidalgo, which ended the war?

_____

_____

_____

_____

MAP 13.5   The Mexican War, 1846–1848

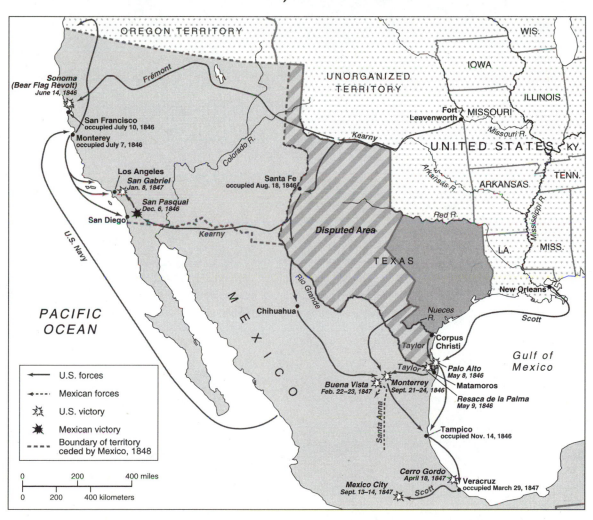

EXPLORING THE MAP

1. The Mexican defeat had huge consequences for Mexico? What were they?

_____

_____

_____

_____

_____

_____

_____

_____

2. How did the military experience of Zachary Taylor, Winfield Scott, and John Frémont affect their political careers?

_____

_____

_____

_____

_____

_____

_____

_____

NOTES

ABRAHAM LINCOLN'S AMERICA
1800–1860

Introduction

By 1860, the United States had expanded from the Atlantic to the Pacific coast. The growth of the nation had profound implications for U.S. development, particularly for how the new territories were organized. Those peoples affected by the expansion also faced severe consequences, the most serious of which was the possible loss of their lands. See *The American Promise*, page 513.

READING THE MAP

1. To place U.S. expansion in perspective, construct a chronology of the acquisition of territory to 1860. Include the date, the name of the region, from whom the land was obtained, and how the United States acquired it. Use the following first entry as a model.

   1803: Louisiana Purchase, France, purchase

   _____

   _____

   _____

   _____

   _____

   _____

   _____

2. Which nation lost the most land from U. S. expansion?

   _____

3. What means proved most effective for acquiring territory—war or diplomacy?

   _____

CONNECTING TO THE CHAPTER

1. The concept of Manifest Destiny strongly influenced U.S. expansion. Who coined the phrase "Manifest Destiny"? When? What does it mean?

   _____

   _____

   _____

   _____

2. The promise of cheap land stimulated movement west. Noting changes over time (between 1800 and 1854), indicate the price the U.S. government charged for an acre of land and the minimum purchase.

   _____

   _____

   _____

   _____

3. The election of 1844 revolved around the issue of U.S. expansion. What areas targeted for expansion were debated during the election campaign? How did the views of the presidential candidates about these areas affect their fortunes in the campaign?

MAP 13.6   *Territorial Expansion by 1860*

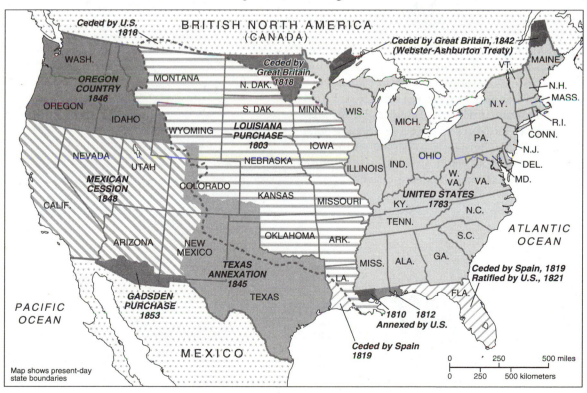

EXPLORING THE MAP

1. Compare Map 13.6 with Map 1.3 on Native Americans. Identify the various Native American peoples affected by U.S. expansion. According to chapter 13, what was the government's attitude toward Native Americans, and what policy regarding Native Americans did the government institute?

2. Overland migration to Oregon and California has been celebrated in books and movies. On a separate piece of paper, write a diary chronicling the experience of a man or a woman on the overland trail from Missouri to Oregon or California. Include such details as where the trip began, various situations encountered on the trail, and emotions on reaching the destination.

3. The quest for religious freedom led the Mormons from New York to Utah. Prepare an advertising flier to promote Mormon settlement in Utah. Include reasons why Mormons should leave the East, descriptions of Utah geography, and positive aspects of Mormon life in Utah.

NOTES

CHAPTER 14

THE HOUSE DIVIDED
1846–1861

Introduction

The increasing tension over settling western territories reached a breaking point in 1854 with the Kansas-Nebraska Act. The goal of the act was to finally resolve the issue of slavery in the territories, but instead it made an already bad situation worse by overturning the carefully planned compromise legislation of the previous thirty-five years. See *The American Promise*, page 534.

READING THE MAP

1. A major political concern was to ensure that neither pro- nor antislavery forces gained an upper hand in Congress, particularly in the Senate. Before 1854, how many slave and how many free states were there?

   _____

   _____

   _____

2. Estimate the percentage of U.S. land occupied by the territories. Given the location of free and slave states, estimate the percentage of territory likely to be settled by slaveholders.

   _____

   _____

   _____

   _____

3. Referring to the answers to questions 1 and 2, consider whether slaveholders or free-soil advocates would be more likely to support changes in government legislation to discontinue the Missouri Compromise, which forbade slavery north of Missouri's southern border? Why?

   _____

   _____

   _____

   _____

   _____

   _____

   _____

   _____

   _____

CONNECTING TO THE CHAPTER

1. For the table on page 100, construct a chronology of the four important pieces of legislation passed or debated on the question of settling the territories. Include the date of passage or debate, the name of each legislative act, and the provisions of each act. Use the boldface entry as a model. Then answer the following question: How did the Kansas-Nebraska Act change U.S. policy on organizing the territories, including the issue of Native American lands?

(Question 1 continues) _____

_____

_____

_____

_____

_____

_____

2. Why did the Kansas-Nebraska Act escalate sectional conflicts? What role did geography play in heightening tensions in the Kansas and Nebraska Territories?

_____

_____

_____

_____

_____

MAP 14.3   *The Kansas-Nebraska Act, 1854*

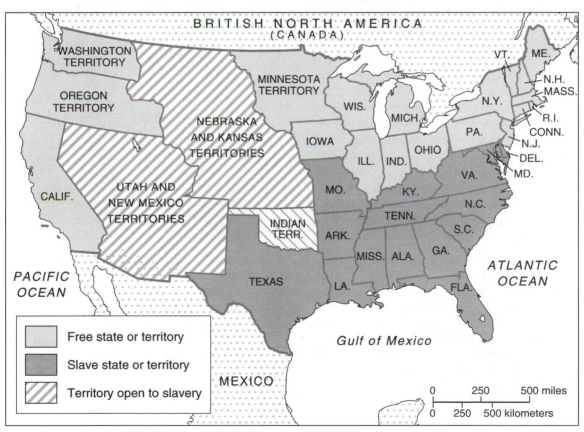

Date	Act	Provisions
1820	Missouri Compromise	Missouri admitted as a slave state, Maine as a free state. Slavery prohibited north of 36°30′ latitude line.

EXPLORING THE MAP

1. A major point of division between slave and free advocates concerned how the presence of one would affect the fortunes of the other. Choose a location in the Kansas and Nebraska Territories to settle. Then make a list of the requirements slave plantation owners would like implemented and a similar list for a free farmer. Include such aspects as the following.

   • Organization and development of the land. Organize the land using the township and range plan of the Northwest Territory (see Map 8.2 in the textbook), which divided the land into townships of thirty-six sections, one of which was devoted to education. How would the land be developed economically?

   • Political development following the laws of the day, which included the stipulation that each slave counted as three-fifths of one person in voting.

   • The social structure of society, including status and class organization.

   Compare the two lists and assess why slave and free-soil advocates could or could not settle a territory together.

NOTES

THE HOUSE DIVIDED
1846–1861

Introduction

In the late 1840s and 1850s, the U.S. political scene was in constant flux as the debate over slave versus free soil, labor, and people intensified, defying resolution. See *The American Promise*, page 536.

PUTTING THE POLITICAL REALIGNMENT IN PERSPECTIVE

Beginning in the late 1840s, the two-party system forged during the 1830s unraveled. Examine the election results between 1848 and 1860 to fill out the following table. Use the boldface entry as a model, underlining the winner in each election. Give the areas of strength for each party, noting where the parties dominated or shared strength. Then answer the questions following the table to help make sense of the political realignment that occurred after 1848.

1. What issue proved so divisive between 1848 and 1860 and what did the debate focus upon?

_____

_____

_____

Year	Candidates, Parties, Winner (underlined)	Areas of Strength
1848	**Taylor, Whig vs. Cass, Democrat**	**Whig: Northeast, middle South; Democrat: Northwest, Southwest; Shared: Southeast**

2. How did the political parties realign them-
   selves in the 1850s?

_____

_____

_____

_____

_____

_____

Map 14.4   Political Realignment, 1848–1860

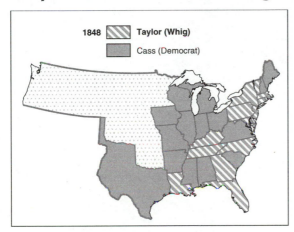

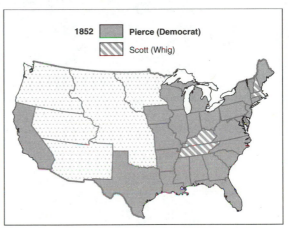

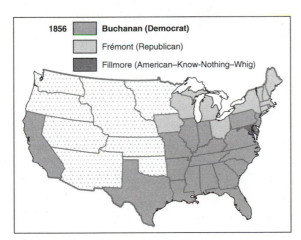

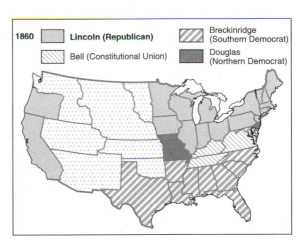

3. Taking account of the growing issues and divisions, write a platform for a new political party that would transcend sections and represent the nation as a whole. Include what the major goals of the party would be, the vision of the future of the nation, and any specific programs to meet these goals and vision.

NOTES

THE CRUCIBLE OF WAR
1861–1865

Introduction

The Civil War pitted two distinctive societies with differing visions of the future against each other. Ironically, both the Union and the Confederacy believed they were fighting to preserve the same democratic heritage, but the war was actually fought over slavery. See *The American Promise*, page 573.

MAKING SENSE OF THE CIVIL WAR, 1861–1862

1. At the outset of the Civil War, both sides were confident of victory. To understand why both North and South thought they would win, use Map 15.2 and chapter 15 to complete the following chart. Then assess which side had a more realistic view of its chances.

Category	North	South
Why they fought		
Potential for victory	1.	1.
	2.	2.
	3.	3.
	4.	4.
	5.	5.
	6.	
	7.	

2. Examine the map and locate the three theaters of war. Using Map 15.2 and chapter 15, assess who was winning in each theater by identifying who was winning more battles or had fewer casualties.

_____

_____

_____

MAP 15.2   The Civil War, 1861–1862

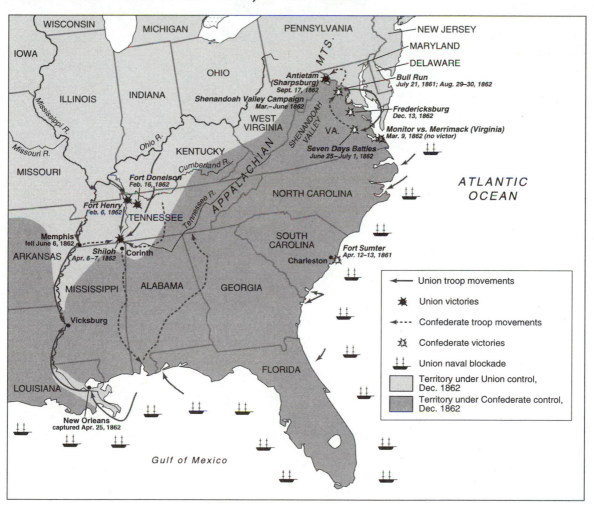

3. A major initiative by the Union was to blockade the South and cut it off from contact with other nations by sea. Why was the North able to blockade the long southern coast? How successful was the blockade? Besides blockading the coast, what else did the North do to curtail southern shipping?

Notes

THE CRUCIBLE OF WAR
1861–1865

Introduction

The last three years of the Civil War saw the tide turn against the Confederacy. The continuing conflict took its toll not only on the military forces of both sides but on the southern land where the campaigns were waged. It is also important to note that women and African Americans played increasingly important roles in the both the Union and the Confederate war efforts. See *The American Promise*, page 591.

READING THE MAP

1. A major factor in the victory of the North was the location of the war. Examine the map and identify where the bulk of the battles were fought. What Confederate states did Union armies fight in or pass through?

_____

_____

_____

_____

_____

_____

2. The North's strategy was to carve the Confederacy into isolated sections. Looking at the routes of the northern armies, determine whether this strategy was successful. Defend your answer by describing how the South was or was not divided.

_____

_____

_____

_____

_____

_____

CONNECTING TO THE CHAPTER

1. When U. S. Grant became the Union commander in chief, he pursued a simple strategy. What was that strategy, and how did Grant implement it?

_____

_____

_____

_____

_____

2. One result of modern combat in the Civil War was an astounding loss of life. What were the human costs of the war for the South and the North?

MAP 15.3   The Civil War, 1863–1865

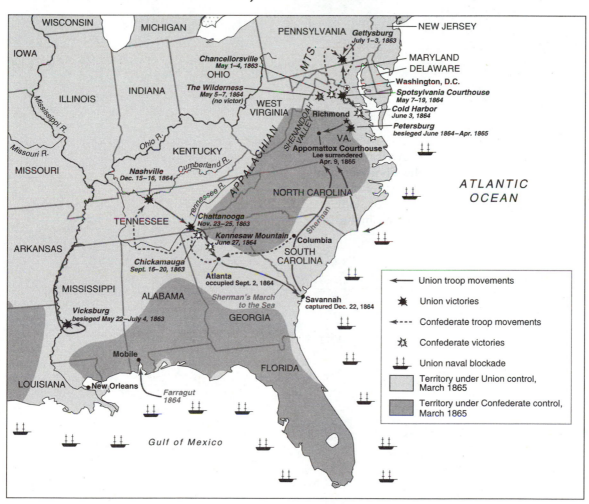

3. How many Southern casualties were there in the Battles of Vicksburg and Gettysburg? In each the following battles, what were the Northern and Southern casualties: Wilderness, Spotsylvania, and Cold Harbor.

_____

_____

_____

_____

_____

_____

_____

_____

_____

EXPLORING THE MAP

1. Assume the identity of an African American slave who served in the Civil War, and write a petition to Congress requesting U.S. citizenship. Include accounts of your efforts to help the Union cause, including combat in battles.

_____

_____

_____

_____

_____

_____

_____

_____

2. Write a journal from the perspective of a woman nurse serving in Union or Confederate hospitals. Include descriptions of the hospital, your daily routine, and the medical care afforded the wounded.

_____

_____

_____

_____

_____

_____

_____

_____

_____

_____

_____

_____

_____

_____

_____

_____

_____

_____

NOTES

CHAPTER 16

RECONSTRUCTION
1863–1877

Introduction

The end of slavery destroyed the foundations of the South's plantation economy. The conditions of the immediate postwar years strongly influenced the rise of a new system based on farm tenancy, and while many things changed, much remained the same for planters and African Americans. See *The American Promise*, page 631.

READING THE MAP

1. Compare and contrast the southern plantation in 1861 and 1881. What remained the same and what changed?

_____

_____

_____

_____

_____

_____

_____

_____

_____

_____

_____

_____

2. Looking at the changes in the layout and structure of the plantations, determine what the freed African Americans gained.

_____

_____

_____

_____

_____

_____

_____

_____

_____

_____

_____

_____

CONNECTING TO THE CHAPTER

Developing a new system of labor and production required accommodating the needs and desires of both planters and African American farmers. Complete the table to compare and contrast their respective needs and desires. Use the boldface entries as a model. Then answer the questions following the table.

	Planters	*African American Farmers*
Landownership		
Labor system		
Personal freedom	Maintain tight control over African Americans: have them remain in clustered houses and limit their personal freedom	

MAP 16.1   A Southern Plantation in 1860 and 1881

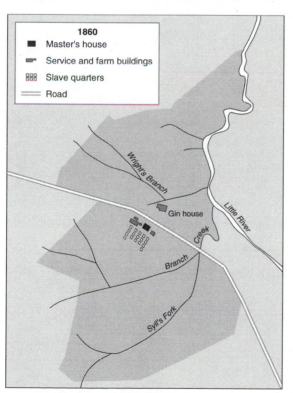
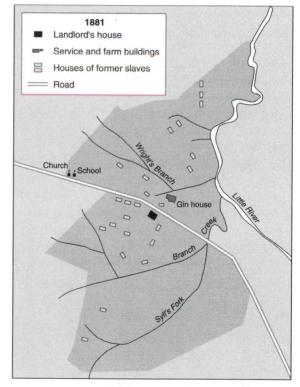

1. In attempting to accommodate the varying needs of planters and labor, what system arose? What prior development influenced its rise?

2. What does it appear that each side gained in the new agricultural system that emerged?

EXPLORING THE MAP

1. From the perspective first of an African American farmer and then of a planter, write two contracts for labor on a southern cotton plantation during Reconstruction. Include specific provisions regarding working conditions and tasks, housing and living conditions, personal freedom and family rights, and payment. Compare a real sharecropping contract to yours. Which of your contracts—African American or planter—is closer to the real one? What does this tell you about power in the South during Reconstruction?

NOTES

RECONSTRUCTION
1863–1877

Introduction

Various groups had differing ideas on how to reconstruct the South. The interplay between these ideas and the programs developed often makes understanding reconstruction difficult. While Map 16.3 contains much information on where reconstruction occurred and when important events happened, this information is just the tip of the iceberg—nine-tenths of the reconstruction story remains hidden. See *The American Promise,* page 636.

PUTTING RECONSTRUCTION IN PERSPECTIVE

1. Using Map 16.3, list in chronological order the readmission of former states to the Union. Then list in chronological order the reestablishment of conservative governments.

MAP 16.3   The Reconstruction of the South

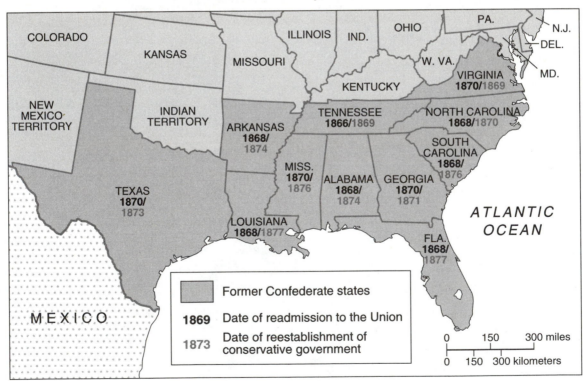

Five Issues	1. **The status and treatment of Confederate government officials and military**
	2.
	3.
	4.
	5.
Three Reconstruction Programs	1. **Lincoln: Swift readmission for national unity. After 10% of the qualified voters in 1860 renounced secession and slavery, state reconstructed.**
	2.
	3.
Acts and Constitutional Amendments	1. **December 1863: Proclamation of Amnesty and Reconstruction (Lincoln plan)**
	2. **July 1864:**
	3. **March 1865:**
	4. **Fall 1865:**
	5. **December 1865:**
	6. **April 1866:**
	7. **June 1866:**
	8. **July 1866:**
	9. **March 1867:**
	10. **February 1869:**

(Question 1 continues) _____

_____

_____

_____

_____

_____

2. Complete the above table, using the bold-face entries as models. Then answer the questions after the table to examine the various Reconstruction programs.

3. What issue did none of the plans address? Why?

_____

_____

4. From the point of view of a white planter or an African American politician/farmer in the South in 1867, write an editorial that critiques the congressional Reconstruction program and offers changes in that program, including provisions for the issue not addressed by the various plans.

5. Assess how well the U.S. Reconstruction program worked. Did it "reconstruct" the nation? Explain your answer.